Exploring Letters

y z zz qu

By James Edward
Illustrated by Q2AMedia
Character illustrations by Jon Stuart

OXFORD
UNIVERSITY PRESS

Listen

💬 TALK

- Explain that all of these words include the /y/ sound. This is the sound made by the letter *y* in the words *yoyo* or *yawn*.

👥 ACTIVITY

- Point to each object and say each word slowly. Ask children to listen for the /y/ sound as you say the words.

- Say the words again, asking children to point to the letter that makes the /y/ sound and to say where it appears in the word (e.g. at the beginning or in the middle). Note that children may not be able to read the whole words at this stage – they are simply identifying an individual sound.

★ Tip

Emphasize the /y/ sound if children find it tricky to hear it in the word. See the inside back cover for more guidance on sounds.

yoghurt

yoyo

yellow

y for yolk

yawn

yolk

3

Write

👥 ACTIVITY

- This is the letter *y*. Explain to children that this is what the /y/ sound looks like when it is written down.
- Ask children to trace the shape of the letter *y* on this page using their writing fingers.
- Then ask children to write the letter *y* in the air with you using their writing fingers.

★ Have some fun!

Using their writing fingers, ask children to write the letter *y* in a tray filled with wet sand or shaving foam, or using water or paint on paper.

4

Sound-talk and blend

ACTIVITY

- Ask children to sound-talk these words – that is, to say the individual sounds – and then blend the sounds together to make a word (e.g. y-e-t becomes yet).
- Encourage children to repeat and practise this activity until they are confident with blending the sounds to make words.

✦ Tip

The dots show one sound made by one letter. The dashes show one sound made by two letters (i.e. the letter l written twice makes one sound /l/).

yap
· · ·

yelp
· · · ·

yum
· · ·

yell
· · —

yes
· · ·

yet
· · ·

Listen

💬 TALK

- Explain that all of these words include the /z/ sound. This is the sound made by the letter *z* in the words *zebra* or *zip*.

👥 ACTIVITY

- Point to each object and say each word slowly. Ask children to listen for the /z/ sound as you say the words.
- Say the words again, asking children to point to the letter that makes the /z/ sound and to say where it appears in the word (e.g. at the beginning or in the middle). Note that children may not be able to read the whole words at this stage – they are simply identifying an individual sound.

⭐ Tip

Emphasize the /z/ sound if children find it tricky to hear it in the word. See the inside back cover for more guidance on sounds.

zebra crossing

ZOO

zoo

zigzag

zebra

z-i-p

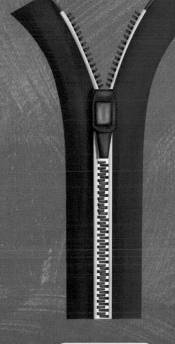

zip

Write

👥 ACTIVITY

- This is the letter *z*. Explain to children that this is what the /z/ sound looks like when it is written down.
- Ask children to trace the shape of the letter *z* on this page using their writing fingers.
- Then ask children to write the letter *z* in the air with you using their writing fingers.

★ Have some fun!

Using their writing fingers, ask children to write the letter *z* in a tray filled with wet sand or shaving foam, or using water or paint on paper.

Sound talk and blend

👥 ACTIVITY

- Ask children to sound-talk these words – that is, to say the individual sounds – and then blend the sounds together to make a word (e.g. z-i-p becomes zip).
- Encourage children to repeat and practise this activity until they are confident with blending the sounds to make words.

★ Tip

The dots show one sound made by one letter.

zigzag
• • • • • •

zip
• • •

zap
• • •

zebra
• • • • •

Listen

💬 TALK

- Sometimes, in words containing the /z/ sound, the letter *z* is written twice (i.e. *zz*) but the sound is still the same.

👥 ACTIVITY

- Point to each object and say each word slowly. Ask children to listen for the /z/ sound as you say the words.

- Say the words again, asking children to point to the letters that make the /z/ sound and to say where they appear in each word (e.g. at the end or in the middle). Note that children may not be able to read the whole words at this stage – they are simply identifying an individual sound.

★ Tip

Emphasize the /z/ sound if children find it tricky to hear it in the word. See the inside back cover for more guidance on sounds.

fi **zz**

si zz le

bu zz

ZZZZZZ

Write

👥 ACTIVITY

- This is *zz*. Explain to children that in some words, the /z/ sound is written like this.
- Ask children to trace the shape of *zz* on this page using their writing fingers.
- Then ask children to write *zz* in the air with you using their writing fingers.

⭐ Have some fun!

Using their writing fingers, ask children to write *zz* in a tray filled with wet sand or shaving foam, or using water or paint on paper.

Sound talk and blend

👥 ACTIVITY

- Ask children to sound-talk these words – that is, to say the individual sounds – and then blend the sounds together to make a word (e.g. j-a-zz becomes jazz).
- Encourage children to repeat and practise this activity until they are confident with blending the sounds to make words.

★ Tip

The dots show one sound made by one letter. The dashes show one sound made by two letters (i.e. the letter *z* written twice makes one sound, /z/).

buzz
• • —

fuzz
• • —

fizz
• • —

frizz
• • • —

jazz
• • —

Listen

🗨 TALK

- Explain that all of these words include the /qu/ sound. This is the sound made by the letters *qu* in the words *quack* or *queen*. This is actually two sounds, /kw/ but it is sensible to think of it as one.

👥 ACTIVITY

- Point to each object and say each word slowly. Ask children to listen for the /qu/ sound as you say the words.

- Say the words again, asking children to point to the letters that make the /qu/ sound and to say where they appear in the word (e.g. at the beginning or in the middle). Note that children may not be able to read the whole words at this stage – they are simply identifying an individual sound.

★ Tip

Emphasize the /qu/ sound if children find it tricky to hear it in the word. See the inside back cover for more guidance on sounds.

quilt

squeak

squelch

queen

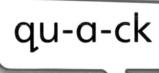
qu-a-ck

quack

Write

ACTIVITY

- This is *qu*. Explain to children that this is what the /qu/ sound looks like when it is written down. In English words, the letter *q* is always followed by letter *u*.
- Ask children to trace the shape of *qu* on this page using their writing fingers.
- Then ask children to write *qu* in the air with you using their writing fingers.

★ **Have some fun!**

Using their writing fingers, ask children to write *qu* in a tray filled with wet sand or shaving foam, or using water or paint on paper.

16

Sound-talk and blend

ACTIVITY

- Ask children to sound-talk these words – that is, to say the individual sounds – and then blend the sounds together to make a word (e.g. qu-i-ck becomes quick).
- Encourage children to repeat and practise this activity until they are confident with blending the sounds to make words.

★ **Tip**

The dots show one sound made by one letter. The dashes show one sound made by two letters (e.g. the letters *qu* make one sound, /qu/).

quiz
— ••

quack
— • —

quit
— ••

quilt
— •••

quick
— •

17

oral blending

👥 **ACTIVITY**

1 Read these short nonsense stories to children.

2 Then read them aloud again. As you read, sound-talk and blend the words in bold – that is, say each sound and then blend the sounds together to make the word (e.g. y-e-ll becomes yell).

3 Ask children to orally repeat the sound-talk and then to blend the sounds together to make the word.
Note that children will not be able to read the text at this stage – this is a speaking and listening activity.

 Tip

Make it fun by adding actions to the words as you sound-talk them. Encourage children to join in!

Yuri likes to eat yellow yoghurt. Yuri will **y-e-ll** 'y-u-ck' if you give her pink yoghurt. She will **y-a-p** 'y-u-m-y-u-m' if the yoghurt is yellow. Yuri has not tried orange yoghurt **y-e-t**. Will she like it? Do you think the answer is **y-e-s** or no? Will she **y-a-p** 'y-u-m-y-u-m' or **y-e-ll** 'y-u-ck'?

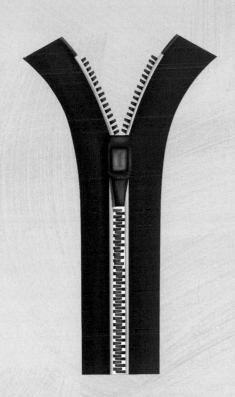

Z-a-k the zebra likes **j-a-zz** music. **Z-e-d** the lion hates **j-a-zz**. **Z-e-d** thinks **j-a-zz** sounds like a **z-i-p** being fastened or the **b-u-zz** of a trapped fly. The jungle starts to **f-i-zz** with the sound of **Z-a-k** and **Z-e-d** arguing. **Z-e-d** ends the argument by eating **Z-a-k**. There is nothing left but the **f-u-zz** of his mane.

Quentin the Duck has a **qu-ee-r** talent. He can get almost every answer right in a **qu-i-z**. He will give a **qu-i-ck qu-a-ck** for 'yes' and two **qu-i-ck qu-a-ck-s** for 'no'. Unfortunately, Quentin is quite a bad loser. If he gets a **qu-i-z** question wrong he spits water at you.

Oral segmenting

👥 ACTIVITY

- Read each of these words to children and then ask them to say the individual sounds in order. So, you say *quiz* and the child says *qu-i-z*.
- If possible, ask children to make the words using magnetic letters or letter cards.

★ EXTENSION

Point to one of the pictures. Ask children to say what it is. Then ask them to say the individual sounds in the word. Note that the pictures are for the following words: *zip*, *buzz* and *quack*.

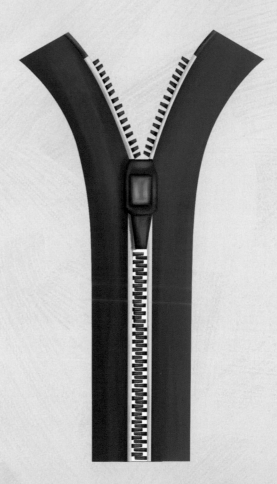

quiz

yuck

yell
:. —

fizz
:. —

Letters and sounds quiz

👥 ACTIVITY

It's time for a quiz!

- Say each of these sounds in a random order, asking children to point to the letter as you say the sound (e.g. Can you point to the letters that make the /qu/ sound?) Remember to say the *sound* of the letter /q/, not the letter name. Ask children to find both examples of the /z/ sound (i.e. *z* and *zz*).
- Now point to each letter and ask children to say both the letter name and the sound that the letter makes.

s c zz

qu a

i y p

Tricky words

- These are words that children will meet a lot in their reading, so it is good to practise them. However, some words have letters which don't sound as children would expect them to. Encourage children to sound-talk as much of the word as they can and help them with the tricky parts.

- Point out the tricky part in the words (i.e. the letter *e* in the words *he* and *she* does not make the /e/ sound as in the word *pen*) and read the words together.

he
●   ●

she
——●